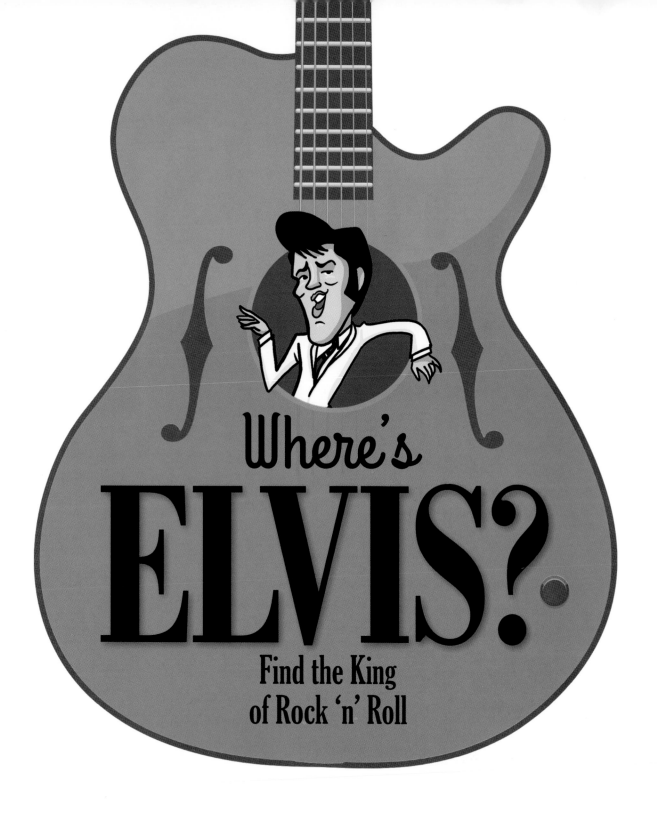

Where's ELVIS?

Find the King
of Rock 'n' Roll

igloobooks

Where's ELVIS?

Can you find the King of Rock 'n' Roll?

Elvis Presley was, quite simply, a superstar. Famous all over the world, he was destined to dramatically change both the sound of popular music and the culture surrounding it. With that sort of responsibility and fame, it would surely not be unreasonable to want to try and adopt a low profile at times. It's all very well and good being an instantly recognizable pioneer of life-changing sounds and a legend of the stage and screen, but no doubt it could become quite tiresome, too! With potentially nowhere for such an iconic performer to hide, we have created scenarios familiar to Elvis for you to seek out the legend. Whether he's lurking behind a chaotic crowd of screaming fans, or looking shady in the corner of a music venue, the King of Rock 'n' Roll remains to be seen, so find him you must!

Where would someone with such megastar status hide? You'd think it would be impossible not to find Elvis among the folks at the famous Memphis Blues Club, but with so much buzz and excitement among guests and musicians, it might have been possible to keep out of sight. So, will the eagle-eyed among you manage to seek him out at such a crowded venue? Binoculars may be in order! Perhaps it would be easier for him to hide within his palatial home, Graceland, during a dazzling, star-studded party? Imagine the eclectic mix of people on the guest list at such an exclusive event! Champagne would be flowing, energetic dancing would be in full swing, and house guests might be spilling out of top-floor windows or rampaging across the beautifully manicured lawns of the Presley's lavish residence. But would Elvis really be able to escape from his fellow party-goers?

Imagine the size of a crowd of excitable, hysterical, female fans queuing up at the studios of the Ed Sullivan Show, desperate to catch a glimpse of their beloved Elvis or touch a spangle from his bright, white suit! Police would have been in attendance, aiming to retain order among the frenzied fans, rendering it possible for Elvis to conceal his glamorous whereabouts. The question is: has Elvis left the building?

How about picturing G.I. Elvis on a visit to a U.S. Army base in West Germany, perhaps, to perform in a concert for the troops! Imagine the scenario, Elvis among a platoon of identically uniformed soldiers, high-security personnel, and fierce guard dogs all in a tightly packed environment where he couldn't possibly stay hidden…or could he?

As we all know, Elvis eventually married his teenage sweetheart, Priscilla, and the wedding would have been a massive occasion on the celebrity calendar. Picture a huge crowd of adoring fans waiting outside the Aladdin Hotel, eager to catch a glimpse of the newlywed lovebirds. Imagine the level of chaos with the paparazzi's cameras flashing at every opportunity, and impatient journalists clutching clipboards and microphones. How could Elvis not be spotted?

Even Elvis liked to take the occasional vacation, and surely the exotic, palm-fringed shores of Hawaii would have beckoned. Imagine a sun-drenched, busy beach scene in Honolulu on this colorful, volcanic island. Countless suntanned, Hawaiian-shirted men and bronzed, bikini-clad women enjoying every aspect of the popular location.

Can you spot Elvis the Pelvis hiding among the high-spirited, vacationing crowds? Impossible, surely?

So, in a coconut shell, here's the brief: try and find the King of Rock 'n' Roll in each bustling scene. Along with that time-consuming, head-scratching, eye-straining mission, there's a curve ball thrown in. We've included some additional hidden celebs and items readily associated with the King.
Thank you very much.

Memphis Blues Club

75893614

Graceland

75893614 0

75893614 0

Dreamboat

758936140

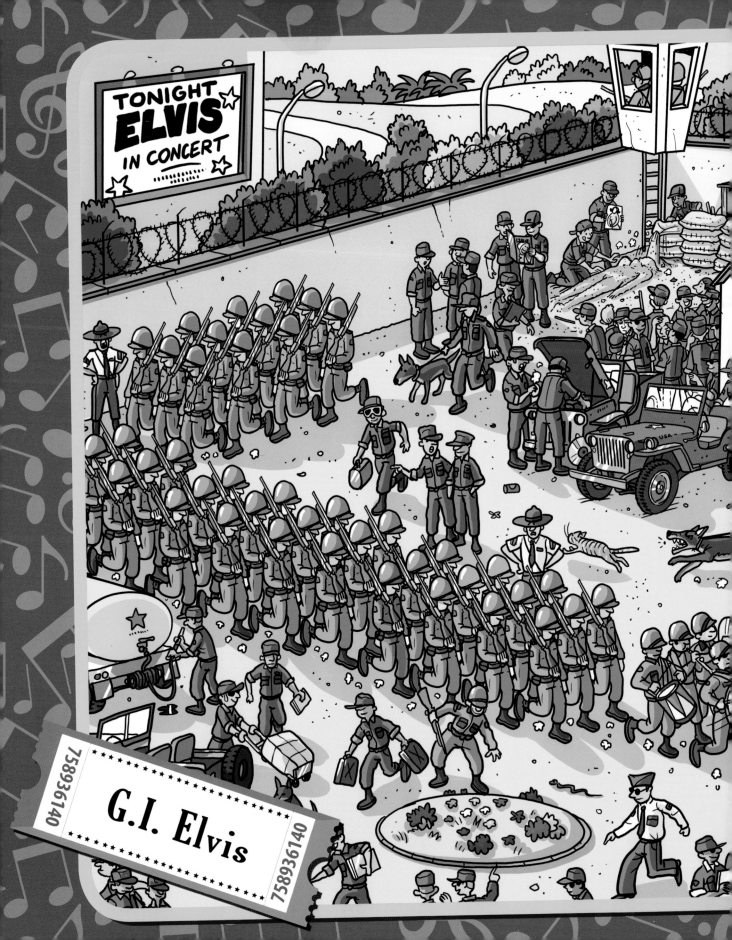

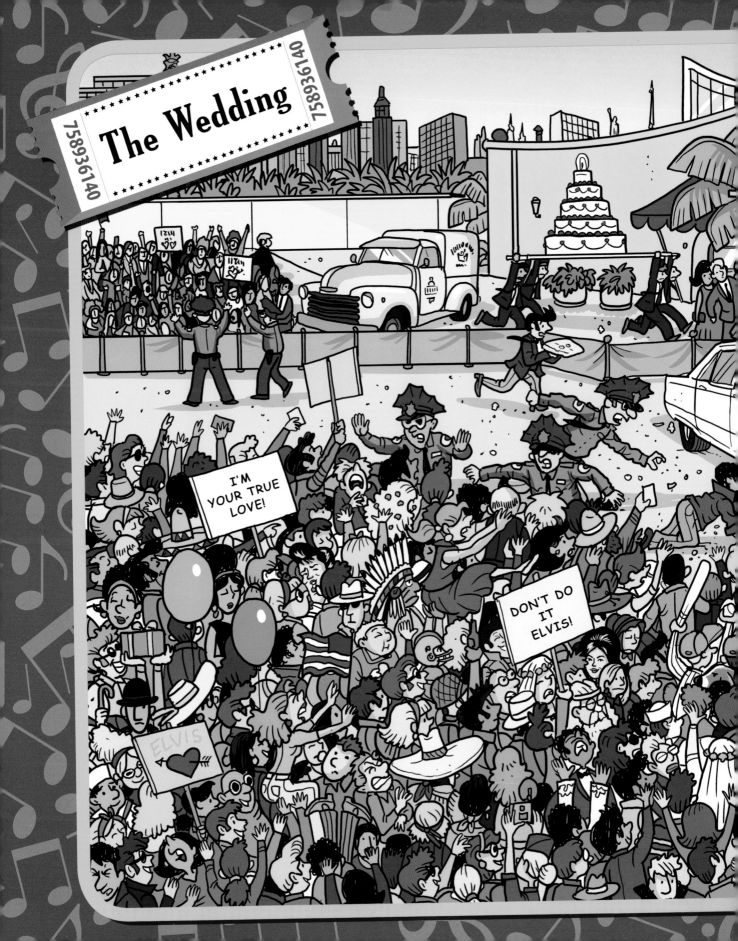

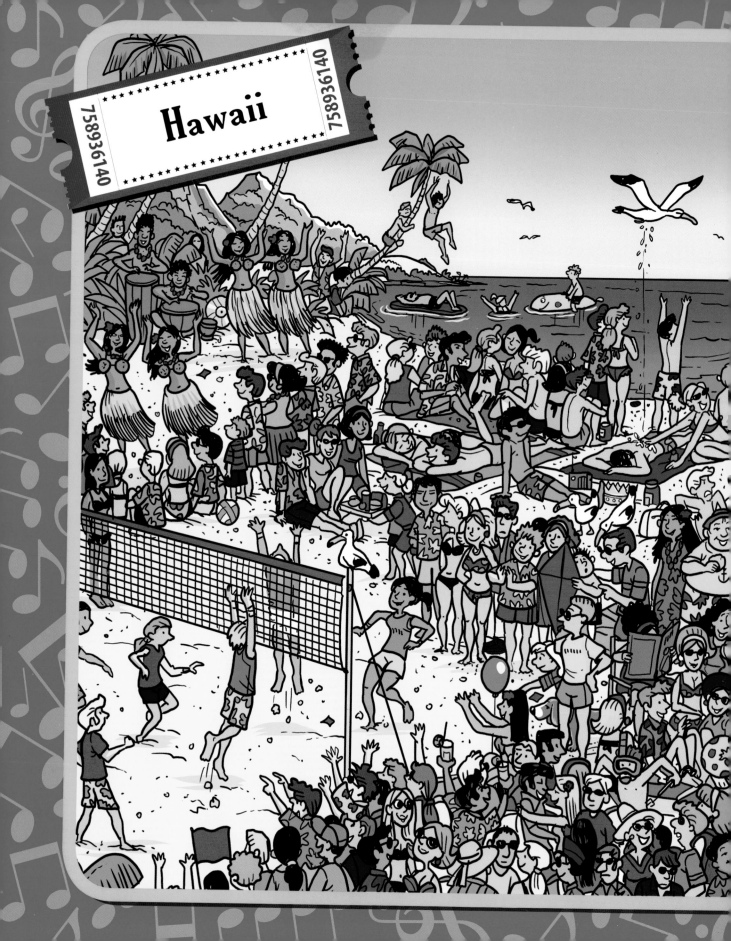

Hawaii

758936140 758936140

Did you also spot...

758936140 758936140

Priscilla Presley — Priscilla was just a teenager when she was first introduced to Elvis. The young sweethearts met in Germany in 1959, and it was love at first sight. They married eight years later.

Sam Phillips — The man behind the music, it was Sam who first spotted the potential and signed Elvis to his recording company, Sun Studio. The rest, as they say, is history…

Lisa Marie Presley — Born in Memphis in February 1968, Lisa Marie, or 'Buttonhead' as Elvis would often call her, was adored by her doting parents.

Colonel Parker — A controversial manager and master dealmaker, Colonel Tom Parker took Elvis' music and movie career to unimaginable heights.

Marilyn Monroe — Movie goddess and Hollywood icon, Marilyn Monroe, will be getting up to her usual mischief. See if you can spot our favorite blond bombshell.

Johnny Cash — In December 1957, the legendary Johnny Cash performed in an impromptu jamming session alongside Elvis, Jerry Lee Lewis, and Carl Perkins at Sun Studio in Memphis.

Frank Sinatra — Famous crooner and movie star, also known as 'Ol' Blue Eyes,' Frank Sinatra and Elvis first performed a duet in 1960.

Tom Jones — When Tom Jones was a teenager, he idolized Elvis. They first met at Paramount Studios in 1965 and later became friends.

B.B. King — Legendary bluesman B.B. King and The King of Rock 'n' Roll shared mutual admiration and respect. The iconic pair notably performed alongside each other at a Memphis fundraising event.

Memphis Mafia — A group of Elvis' close and trusted friends. The term 'Memphis Mafia' was coined by a newspaper reporter when they were first seen wearing respectable dark, mohair suits, resembling a mafia mob.